THIS PLANNER BELONGS TO:

2023 AT A GLANCE

JANUARY 2023

S	M	T	W	T	F	S
1	2	3	4	5	6	7
8	9	10	11	12	13	14
15	16	17	18	19	20	21
22	23	24	25	26	27	28
29	30	31				

FEBRUARY 2023

S	M	T	W	T	F	S
			1	2	3	4
5	6	7	8	9	10	11
12	13	14	15	16	17	18
19	20	21	22	23	24	25
26	27	28				

MARCH 2023

S	M	T	W	T	F	S
			1	2	3	4
5	6	7	8	9	10	11
12	13	14	15	16	17	18
19	20	21	22	23	24	25
26	27	28	29	30	31	

APRIL 2023

S	M	T	W	T	F	S
						1
2	3	4	5	6	7	8
9	10	11	12	13	14	15
16	17	18	19	20	21	22
23/30	24	25	26	27	28	29

MAY 2023

S	M	T	W	T	F	S
	1	2	3	4	5	6
7	8	9	10	11	12	13
14	15	16	17	18	19	20
21	22	23	24	25	26	27
28	29	30	31			

JUNE 2023

S	M	T	W	T	F	S
				1	2	3
4	5	6	7	8	9	10
11	12	13	14	15	16	17
18	19	20	21	22	23	24
25	26	27	28	29	30	

JULY 2023

S	M	T	W	T	F	S
						1
2	3	4	5	6	7	8
9	10	11	12	13	14	15
16	17	18	19	20	21	22
23/30	24/31	25	26	27	28	29

AUGUST 2023

S	M	T	W	T	F	S
		1	2	3	4	5
6	7	8	9	10	11	12
13	14	15	16	17	18	19
20	21	22	23	24	25	26
27	28	29	30	31		

SEPTEMBER 2023

S	M	T	W	T	F	S
					1	2
3	4	5	6	7	8	9
10	11	12	13	14	15	16
17	18	19	20	21	22	23
24	25	26	27	28	29	30

OCTOBER 2023

S	M	T	W	T	F	S
1	2	3	4	5	6	7
8	9	10	11	12	13	14
15	16	17	18	19	20	21
22	23	24	25	26	27	28
29	30	31				

NOVEMBER 2023

S	M	T	W	T	F	S
			1	2	3	4
5	6	7	8	9	10	11
12	13	14	15	16	17	18
19	20	21	22	23	24	25
26	27	28	29	30		

DECEMBER 2023

S	M	T	W	T	F	S
					1	2
3	4	5	6	7	8	9
10	11	12	13	14	15	16
17	18	19	20	21	22	23
24/31	25	26	27	28	29	30

2024 AT A GLANCE

JANUARY 2024

S	M	T	W	T	F	S
	1	2	3	4	5	6
7	8	9	10	11	12	13
14	15	16	17	18	19	20
21	22	23	24	25	26	27
28	29	30	31			

FEBRUARY 2024

S	M	T	W	T	F	S
				1	2	3
4	5	6	7	8	9	10
11	12	13	14	15	16	17
18	19	20	21	22	23	24
25	26	27	28	29		

MARCH 2024

S	M	T	W	T	F	S
					1	2
3	4	5	6	7	8	9
10	11	12	13	14	15	16
17	18	19	20	21	22	23
24/31	25	26	27	28	29	30

APRIL 2024

S	M	T	W	T	F	S
	1	2	3	4	5	6
7	8	9	10	11	12	13
14	15	16	17	18	19	20
21	22	23	24	25	26	27
28	29	30				

MAY 2024

S	M	T	W	T	F	S
			1	2	3	4
5	6	7	8	9	10	11
12	13	14	15	16	17	18
19	20	21	22	23	24	25
26	27	28	29	30	31	

JUNE 2024

S	M	T	W	T	F	S
						1
2	3	4	5	6	7	8
9	10	11	12	13	14	15
16	17	18	19	20	21	22
23/30	24	25	26	27	28	29

JULY 2024

S	M	T	W	T	F	S
	1	2	3	4	5	6
7	8	9	10	11	12	13
14	15	16	17	18	19	20
21	22	23	24	25	26	27
28	29	30	31			

AUGUST 2024

S	M	T	W	T	F	S
				1	2	3
4	5	6	7	8	9	10
11	12	13	14	15	16	17
18	19	20	21	22	23	24
25	26	27	28	29	30	31

SEPTEMBER 2024

S	M	T	W	T	F	S
1	2	3	4	5	6	7
8	9	10	11	12	13	14
15	16	17	18	19	20	21
22	23	24	25	26	27	28
29	30					

OCTOBER 2024

S	M	T	W	T	F	S
		1	2	3	4	5
6	7	8	9	10	11	12
13	14	15	16	17	18	19
20	21	22	23	24	25	26
27	28	29	30	31		

NOVEMBER 2024

S	M	T	W	T	F	S
					1	2
3	4	5	6	7	8	9
10	11	12	13	14	15	16
17	18	19	20	21	22	23
24	25	26	27	28	29	30

DECEMBER 2024

S	M	T	W	T	F	S
1	2	3	4	5	6	7
8	9	10	11	12	13	14
15	16	17	18	19	20	21
22	23	24	25	26	27	28
29	30	31				

MONTHLY GOALS

NEW GOALS TO FOCUS ON

WHAT WORKED LAST MONTH

WHAT COULD BE BETTER

Bloom
and
Grow

AUGUST 2023

SUNDAY	MONDAY	TUESDAY	WEDNESDAY	THURSDAY	FRIDAY	SATURDAY
30	31	1	2	3	4	5
6	7 Summer Bank Holiday (SCT)	8	9	10	11	12
13	14	15	16	17	18	19
20	21	22	23	24	25	26
27	28 Summer Bank Holiday	29	30	31	1	2

CREATURE OF HABIT

Track new goals or habits and watch your progress every month!

HABIT	1	2	3	4	5	6	7	8	9	10	11	12	13	14	15	16	17	18	19	20	21	22	23	24	25	26	27	28	29	30	31

2023 JULY/AUGUST

MONDAY
31

DO MORE OF WHAT MAKES YOU HAPPY

TUESDAY
1

WEDNESDAY
2

DON'T JUST SURVIVE, *THRIVE*.

THURSDAY
3

BREAKING NEWS: YOU'RE MARVELOUS!

FRIDAY
4

SATURDAY
5

SUNDAY
6

WHAT'S SOMETHING TO BE EXCITED ABOUT TODAY? IS IT YOU?

DON'T FORGET:

AUGUST 2023

S	M	T	W	T	F	S
		1	2	3	4	5
6	7	8	9	10	11	12
13	14	15	16	17	18	19
20	21	22	23	24	25	26
27	28	29	30	31		

SEPTEMBER 2023

S	M	T	W	T	F	S
					1	2
3	4	5	6	7	8	9
10	11	12	13	14	15	16
17	18	19	20	21	22	23
24	25	26	27	28	29	30

THIS WEEK'S HAPPY MOMENT:

2023 **AUGUST**

MONDAY
7

Summer Bank Holiday (SCT)

TUESDAY
8

POSITIVE VIBES + MAXIMUM EFFORT = ***NO LIMITS!***

WEDNESDAY
9

THURSDAY
10

TREAT YOURSELF LIKE A HOUSEPLANT:
WITH PLENTY OF WATER AND LOTS OF SUN.

FRIDAY
11

TAKE TIME TO
JUST CHILL.

SATURDAY
12

SUNDAY
13

DON'T FORGET:

THIS WEEK'S
HAPPY MOMENT:

AUGUST 2023

S	M	T	W	T	F	S
		1	2	3	4	5
6	7	8	9	10	11	12
13	14	15	16	17	18	19
20	21	22	23	24	25	26
27	28	29	30	31		

SEPTEMBER 2023

S	M	T	W	T	F	S
					1	2
3	4	5	6	7	8	9
10	11	12	13	14	15	16
17	18	19	20	21	22	23
24	25	26	27	28	29	30

2023 **AUGUST**

MONDAY
14

SMILE, SHINE, SHOW 'EM WHO'S BOSS!

TUESDAY
15

WEDNESDAY
16

REMEMBER: YOU HAVE TO BE A BEGINNER BEFORE ANYTHING ELSE.

THURSDAY
17

CRACK YOURSELF UP TODAY!

FRIDAY
18

SATURDAY
19

IT'S THE WEEKEND!
EASY DOES IT.

SUNDAY
20

DON'T FORGET:

AUGUST 2023

S	M	T	W	T	F	S
		1	2	3	4	5
6	7	8	9	10	11	12
13	14	15	16	17	18	19
20	21	22	23	24	25	26
27	28	29	30	31		

SEPTEMBER 2023

S	M	T	W	T	F	S
					1	2
3	4	5	6	7	8	9
10	11	12	13	14	15	16
17	18	19	20	21	22	23
24	25	26	27	28	29	30

THIS WEEK'S
HAPPY MOMENT:

2023 **AUGUST**

MONDAY
21

TUESDAY
22

FOLLOW YOUR DREAMS.
THEY KNOW THE WAY!

WEDNESDAY
23

THURSDAY
24

BEING HAPPY NEVER GOES
OUT OF STYLE. FLAUNT IT!

FRIDAY
25

TAKE UP ALL THE
SPACE YOU DESERVE.

SATURDAY
26

SUNDAY
27

DON'T FORGET:

AUGUST 2023

S	M	T	W	T	F	S
		1	2	3	4	5
6	7	8	9	10	11	12
13	14	15	16	17	18	19
20	21	22	23	24	25	26
27	28	29	30	31		

SEPTEMBER 2023

S	M	T	W	T	F	S
					1	2
3	4	5	6	7	8	9
10	11	12	13	14	15	16
17	18	19	20	21	22	23
24	25	26	27	28	29	30

THIS WEEK'S
HAPPY MOMENT:

MONDAY
28

REPEAT: I AM BIGGER THAN MY FEARS.

Summer Bank Holiday (UK except SCT)

TUESDAY
29

WEDNESDAY
30

CELEBRATE A LITTLE SOMETHING EVERY DAY!

THURSDAY
31

DREAM IT. BELIEVE IT. ACHIEVE IT.

FRIDAY
1

SATURDAY
2

SUNDAY FUN DAY! MEET UP WITH A FRIEND AND PAMPER YOURSELVES.

SUNDAY
3

Father's Day (AUS, NZ)

DON'T FORGET:

THIS WEEK'S HAPPY MOMENT:

AUGUST 2023

S	M	T	W	T	F	S
		1	2	3	4	5
6	7	8	9	10	11	12
13	14	15	16	17	18	19
20	21	22	23	24	25	26
27	28	29	30	31		

SEPTEMBER 2023

S	M	T	W	T	F	S
					1	2
3	4	5	6	7	8	9
10	11	12	13	14	15	16
17	18	19	20	21	22	23
24	25	26	27	28	29	30

MONTHLY GOALS

NEW GOALS TO FOCUS ON

WHAT WORKED LAST MONTH

WHAT COULD BE BETTER

DON'T STOP CHASING THE LIGHT

SEPTEMBER 2023

SUNDAY	MONDAY	TUESDAY	WEDNESDAY	THURSDAY	FRIDAY	SATURDAY
27	28	29	30	31	1	2
3 Father's Day (AUS, NZ)	4 Labor Day (USA, CAN)	5	6	7	8	9
10	11 Patriot Day	12	13	14	15 Rosh Hashanah begins	16
17	18	19	20	21	22	23 Autumn begins (Northern Hemisphere)
24	25	26	27	28	29	30

CREATURE OF HABIT

Track new goals or habits and watch your progress every month!

HABIT	1	2	3	4	5	6	7	8	9	10	11	12	13	14	15	16	17	18	19	20	21	22	23	24	25	26	27	28	29	30	31

2023 SEPTEMBER

MONDAY
4

Labor Day (USA, CAN)

TUESDAY
5

GOOD VIBES ARE COMING YOUR WAY! PASS THEM ON.

WEDNESDAY
6

THURSDAY
7

YOUR FUTURE IS BRIGHTER THAN THE SUN.

FRIDAY
8

UNPLUG FROM TECHNOLOGY TODAY AND GO PLAY!

SATURDAY
9

SUNDAY
10

DON'T FORGET:

SEPTEMBER 2023

S	M	T	W	T	F	S
					1	2
3	4	5	6	7	8	9
10	11	12	13	14	15	16
17	18	19	20	21	22	23
24	25	26	27	28	29	30

OCTOBER 2023

S	M	T	W	T	F	S
1	2	3	4	5	6	7
8	9	10	11	12	13	14
15	16	17	18	19	20	21
22	23	24	25	26	27	28
29	30	31				

THIS WEEK'S HAPPY MOMENT:

2023 SEPTEMBER

MONDAY
11

LOVING YOURSELF COSTS NOTHING, BUT IN THE PROCESS, YOU GAIN EVERYTHING.

Patriot Day

TUESDAY
12

WEDNESDAY
13

KEEP KILLING IT. YOU'RE ON A ROLL!

THURSDAY
14

THIS IS YOUR TAKE-A-BREAK
COUPON. USE AS NEEDED.

FRIDAY 15

Rosh Hashanah begins

SATURDAY 16

THE BEST IS
YET TO COME.

SUNDAY 17

DON'T FORGET:

THIS WEEK'S
HAPPY MOMENT:

SEPTEMBER 2023

S	M	T	W	T	F	S
					1	2
3	4	5	6	7	8	9
10	11	12	13	14	15	16
17	18	19	20	21	22	23
24	25	26	27	28	29	30

OCTOBER 2023

S	M	T	W	T	F	S
1	2	3	4	5	6	7
8	9	10	11	12	13	14
15	16	17	18	19	20	21
22	23	24	25	26	27	28
29	30	31				

2023 SEPTEMBER

MONDAY
18

TUESDAY
19

DON'T QUIT YOUR DAYDREAM.

WEDNESDAY
20

THURSDAY
21

GIVE A STRANGER A COMPLIMENT.
YOU'LL BOTH FEEL GREAT!

FRIDAY
22

NEVER MISS A
CHANCE TO DANCE.

SATURDAY
23

Autumn begins (Northern Hemisphere)

SUNDAY
24

Yom Kippur begins

DON'T FORGET:

SEPTEMBER 2023

S	M	T	W	T	F	S
					1	2
3	4	5	6	7	8	9
10	11	12	13	14	15	16
17	18	19	20	21	22	23
24	25	26	27	28	29	30

OCTOBER 2023

S	M	T	W	T	F	S
1	2	3	4	5	6	7
8	9	10	11	12	13	14
15	16	17	18	19	20	21
22	23	24	25	26	27	28
29	30	31				

THIS WEEK'S
HAPPY MOMENT:

2023 **SEPTEMBER/OCTOBER**

MONDAY
25

NO ONE EVER HURT THEIR EYES BY LOOKING ON THE BRIGHT SIDE!

TUESDAY
26

WEDNESDAY
27

TO DO TODAY: LIVE IN THE MOMENT.

THURSDAY
28

TELL SOMEONE A GOOD JOKE. LIFE IS BETTER WHEN YOU'RE LAUGHING!

FRIDAY 29

Sukkot begins

SATURDAY 30

YOU'RE DOING BETTER THAN YOU THINK.

SUNDAY 1

DON'T FORGET:

SEPTEMBER 2023

S	M	T	W	T	F	S
					1	2
3	4	5	6	7	8	9
10	11	12	13	14	15	16
17	18	19	20	21	22	23
24	25	26	27	28	29	30

OCTOBER 2023

S	M	T	W	T	F	S
1	2	3	4	5	6	7
8	9	10	11	12	13	14
15	16	17	18	19	20	21
22	23	24	25	26	27	28
29	30	31				

THIS WEEK'S HAPPY MOMENT:

MONTHLY GOALS

NEW GOALS TO FOCUS ON

WHAT WORKED LAST MONTH

WHAT COULD BE BETTER

HAPPINESS
comes in
WAVES

OCTOBER 2023

SUNDAY	MONDAY	TUESDAY	WEDNESDAY	THURSDAY	FRIDAY	SATURDAY
1	2	3	4	5	6	7
8	9 Columbus Day (USA); Indigenous Peoples' Day (USA); Thanksgiving Day (CAN)	10	11	12	13	14
15	16	17	18	19	20	21
22	23	24	25	26	27	28
29	30	31	1	2	3	4

CREATURE OF HABIT

Track new goals or habits and watch your progress every month!

HABIT	1	2	3	4	5	6	7	8	9	10	11	12	13	14	15	16	17	18	19	20	21	22	23	24	25	26	27	28	29	30	31

2023 **OCTOBER**

MONDAY
2

TUESDAY
3

WHAT SHOULD YOU DO TODAY?
SMILE. SMILE A LOT.

WEDNESDAY
4

THURSDAY
5

IT'S PUMPKIN MONTH! BE INTENTIONAL
AND CARVE OUT TIME FOR YOURSELF.

FRIDAY
6

WE ALL HAVE A LITTLE BIT OF MAGIC INSIDE US.

SATURDAY
7

SUNDAY
8

DON'T FORGET:

OCTOBER 2023

S	M	T	W	T	F	S
1	2	3	4	5	6	7
8	9	10	11	12	13	14
15	16	17	18	19	20	21
22	23	24	25	26	27	28
29	30	31				

NOVEMBER 2023

S	M	T	W	T	F	S
			1	2	3	4
5	6	7	8	9	10	11
12	13	14	15	16	17	18
19	20	21	22	23	24	25
26	27	28	29	30		

THIS WEEK'S HAPPY MOMENT:

2023 **OCTOBER**

MONDAY
9

YOU *ARE* A SUCCESS, EVEN IF
YOU DON'T ALWAYS FEEL IT!

Columbus Day (USA); Indigenous Peoples' Day (USA); Thanksgiving Day (CAN)

TUESDAY
10

WEDNESDAY
11

DOGS CAN BOOST YOUR
HAPPY LEVELS. PET A PUPPY

THURSDAY
12

YOU AND JOY ARE LIKE
TWO PEAS IN A POD!

FRIDAY
13

SATURDAY
14

YOUR ADVENTURE
AWAITS!

SUNDAY
15

DON'T FORGET:

OCTOBER 2023

S	M	T	W	T	F	S
1	2	3	4	5	6	7
8	9	10	11	12	13	14
15	16	17	18	19	20	21
22	23	24	25	26	27	28
29	30	31				

NOVEMBER 2023

S	M	T	W	T	F	S
			1	2	3	4
5	6	7	8	9	10	11
12	13	14	15	16	17	18
19	20	21	22	23	24	25
26	27	28	29	30		

THIS WEEK'S
HAPPY MOMENT:

2023 **OCTOBER**

MONDAY
16

TUESDAY
17

LEAVES ARE FALLING, AND AUTUMN IS CALLING! SAVOR IT.

WEDNESDAY
18

THURSDAY
19

SIMPLE THINGS CAN STILL BE SIGNIFICANT.

FRIDAY
20

YOU'RE COOLER
THAN A CUCUMBER.

SATURDAY
21

SUNDAY
22

DON'T FORGET:

OCTOBER 2023

S	M	T	W	T	F	S
1	2	3	4	5	6	7
8	9	10	11	12	13	14
15	16	17	18	19	20	21
22	23	24	25	26	27	28
29	30	31				

NOVEMBER 2023

S	M	T	W	T	F	S
			1	2	3	4
5	6	7	8	9	10	11
12	13	14	15	16	17	18
19	20	21	22	23	24	25
26	27	28	29	30		

THIS WEEK'S
HAPPY MOMENT:

2023 **OCTOBER**

MONDAY
23

WAKE UP, STRETCH, AND
START YOUR DAY OFF RIGHT!

TUESDAY
24

WEDNESDAY
25

BE CUTE. BE TOUGH. BE WEIRD.
BE HAPPY. JUST BE YOU!

THURSDAY
26

THE BEST TEAM TO BE ON IS YOURS.

FRIDAY 27

SATURDAY 28

GIVE YOURSELF THE ROYAL TREATMENT EVERY DAY.

SUNDAY 29

DON'T FORGET:

OCTOBER 2023

S	M	T	W	T	F	S
1	2	3	4	5	6	7
8	9	10	11	12	13	14
15	16	17	18	19	20	21
22	23	24	25	26	27	28
29	30	31				

NOVEMBER 2023

S	M	T	W	T	F	S
			1	2	3	4
5	6	7	8	9	10	11
12	13	14	15	16	17	18
19	20	21	22	23	24	25
26	27	28	29	30		

THIS WEEK'S HAPPY MOMENT:

MONTHLY GOALS

NEW GOALS TO FOCUS ON

WHAT WORKED LAST MONTH

WHAT COULD BE BETTER

IF YOU
STUMBLE
MAKE IT
PART
OF THE
DANCE

NOVEMBER 2023

SUNDAY	MONDAY	TUESDAY	WEDNESDAY	THURSDAY	FRIDAY	SATURDAY
29	30	31	1	2	3	4
5 Daylight Saving Time ends (USA, CAN)	6	7 Election Day	8	9	10	11 Veterans Day (USA); Remembrance Day (CAN, UK)
12 Diwali begins	13	14	15	16	17	18
19	20	21	22	23 Thanksgiving Day	24	25
26	27	28	29	30 St. Andrew's Day (SCT)	1	2

CREATURE OF HABIT

Track new goals or habits and watch your progress every month!

HABIT	1	2	3	4	5	6	7	8	9	10	11	12	13	14	15	16	17	18	19	20	21	22	23	24	25	26	27	28	29	30	31

MONDAY
30

TUESDAY
31

NORMAL IS OVERRATED.
HOW WILL YOU BE ***UNIQUE***?

Halloween

WEDNESDAY
1

THURSDAY
2

LIVE MORE, WORRY LESS.

FRIDAY
3

SATURDAY
4

PROCRASTINATION WEEKEND! MOVE SOMETHING TO MONDAY!

SUNDAY
5

Daylight Saving Time ends (USA, CAN)

DON'T FORGET:

NOVEMBER 2023

S	M	T	W	T	F	S
			1	2	3	4
5	6	7	8	9	10	11
12	13	14	15	16	17	18
19	20	21	22	23	24	25
26	27	28	29	30		

DECEMBER 2023

S	M	T	W	T	F	S
					1	2
3	4	5	6	7	8	9
10	11	12	13	14	15	16
17	18	19	20	21	22	23
24/31	25	26	27	28	29	30

THIS WEEK'S HAPPY MOMENT:

2023 NOVEMBER

MONDAY
6

GIVE UP THE THINGS THAT WEIGH
YOU DOWN IN ORDER TO FLY.

TUESDAY
7

Election Day

WEDNESDAY
8

THERE ARE MORE ROADS TO THE
TOP OF THE MOUNTAIN THAN
WE EVER THOUGHT POSSIBLE.

THURSDAY
9

PHEW, WHAT A WEEK. BUT YOU MADE IT, AND THAT'S A WIN!

FRIDAY 10

SATURDAY 11

Veterans Day (USA); Remembrance Day (CAN, UK)

ALL ABOARD THE POSITIVITY TRAIN!

SUNDAY 12

Diwali begins

DON'T FORGET:

NOVEMBER 2023

S	M	T	W	T	F	S
			1	2	3	4
5	6	7	8	9	10	11
12	13	14	15	16	17	18
19	20	21	22	23	24	25
26	27	28	29	30		

DECEMBER 2023

S	M	T	W	T	F	S
					1	2
3	4	5	6	7	8	9
10	11	12	13	14	15	16
17	18	19	20	21	22	23
24/31	25	26	27	28	29	30

THIS WEEK'S HAPPY MOMENT:

2023 **NOVEMBER**

MONDAY
13

TUESDAY
14

WHAT FILLS UP YOUR JOY JAR
TREAT YOURSELF THIS WEEK

WEDNESDAY
15

THURSDAY
16

ALWAYS REMEMBER: *MAKE IT FUN*

FRIDAY
17

TOO FAB TO BE DRAB.

SATURDAY
18

SUNDAY
19

DON'T FORGET:

NOVEMBER 2023

S	M	T	W	T	F	S
			1	2	3	4
5	6	7	8	9	10	11
12	13	14	15	16	17	18
19	20	21	22	23	24	25
26	27	28	29	30		

DECEMBER 2023

S	M	T	W	T	F	S
					1	2
3	4	5	6	7	8	9
10	11	12	13	14	15	16
17	18	19	20	21	22	23
24/31	25	26	27	28	29	30

THIS WEEK'S
HAPPY MOMENT:

2023 **NOVEMBER**

MONDAY
20

STOCK UP FOR WINTER: BLANKETS, BOOKS, COCOA, COOKIES.

TUESDAY
21

WEDNESDAY
22

LIVE WITH AN OPEN HEART! WHAT ARE YOU THANKFUL FOR?

THURSDAY
23

Thanksgiving Day

LAUGHTER IS THE BEST MEDICINE. TRY IT OUT!

FRIDAY 24

SATURDAY 25

LIVE AND *LOVE* TO THE FULLEST!

SUNDAY 26

DON'T FORGET:

NOVEMBER 2023

S	M	T	W	T	F	S
			1	2	3	4
5	6	7	8	9	10	11
12	13	14	15	16	17	18
19	20	21	22	23	24	25
26	27	28	29	30		

DECEMBER 2023

S	M	T	W	T	F	S
					1	2
3	4	5	6	7	8	9
10	11	12	13	14	15	16
17	18	19	20	21	22	23
24/31	25	26	27	28	29	30

THIS WEEK'S HAPPY MOMENT:

MONDAY
27

TUESDAY
28

PAT YOURSELF ON THE BACK FOR BEING SO AMAZING!

WEDNESDAY
29

THURSDAY
30

CALL A PAL JUST TO LISTEN AND LET THEM KNOW YOU APPRECIATE THEM.

St. Andrew's Day (SCT)

FRIDAY
1

DEDICATE THIS WEEKEND TO REJUVENATION.

SATURDAY
2

SUNDAY
3

DON'T FORGET:

THIS WEEK'S HAPPY MOMENT:

NOVEMBER 2023

S	M	T	W	T	F	S
			1	2	3	4
5	6	7	8	9	10	11
12	13	14	15	16	17	18
19	20	21	22	23	24	25
26	27	28	29	30		

DECEMBER 2023

S	M	T	W	T	F	S
					1	2
3	4	5	6	7	8	9
10	11	12	13	14	15	16
17	18	19	20	21	22	23
24/31	25	26	27	28	29	30

MONTHLY GOALS

NEW GOALS TO FOCUS ON

WHAT WORKED LAST MONTH

WHAT COULD BE BETTER

It always seems impossible until it is done

DECEMBER 2023

SUNDAY	MONDAY	TUESDAY	WEDNESDAY	THURSDAY	FRIDAY	SATURDAY
26	27	28	29	30	1	2
3	4	5	6	7 Hanukkah begins; Pearl Harbor Day	8	9
10	11	12	13	14	15	16
17	18	19	20	21 Winter begins (Northern Hemisphere)	22	23
24/31 Christmas Eve (24th); New Year's Eve (31st)	25 Christmas Day	26 Kwanzaa begins; Boxing Day (AUS, CAN, NZ, UK)	27	28	29	30

CREATURE OF HABIT

Track new goals or habits and watch your progress every month!

HABIT	1	2	3	4	5	6	7	8	9	10	11	12	13	14	15	16	17	18	19	20	21	22	23	24	25	26	27	28	29	30	31

2023 DECEMBER

MONDAY
4

'TIS THE SEASON TO BE JOYFUL!

TUESDAY
5

WEDNESDAY
6

YOU HAVE COME SO FAR!

THURSDAY
7

Hanukkah begins; Pearl Harbor Day

STRETCH YOUR MIND AND FLY!

FRIDAY
8

SATURDAY
9

ADD COOL NEW EXPERIENCES TO YOUR COLLECTION.

SUNDAY
10

DON'T FORGET:

DECEMBER 2023

S	M	T	W	T	F	S
					1	2
3	4	5	6	7	8	9
10	11	12	13	14	15	16
17	18	19	20	21	22	23
24/31	25	26	27	28	29	30

JANUARY 2024

S	M	T	W	T	F	S
	1	2	3	4	5	6
7	8	9	10	11	12	13
14	15	16	17	18	19	20
21	22	23	24	25	26	27
28	29	30	31			

THIS WEEK'S HAPPY MOMENT:

2023 DECEMBER

MONDAY
11

TUESDAY
12

MAYBE NOT PERFECT,
DEFINITELY LIMITED EDITION.

WEDNESDAY
13

THURSDAY
14

HOW WILL YOU SHOW
YOUR COURAGE TODAY?

FRIDAY
15

WELCOME TO LOUNGE TOWN! PJS AND COZINESS REQUIRED.

SATURDAY
16

SUNDAY
17

DON'T FORGET:

THIS WEEK'S HAPPY MOMENT:

DECEMBER 2023

S	M	T	W	T	F	S
					1	2
3	4	5	6	7	8	9
10	11	12	13	14	15	16
17	18	19	20	21	22	23
24/31	25	26	27	28	29	30

JANUARY 2024

S	M	T	W	T	F	S
	1	2	3	4	5	6
7	8	9	10	11	12	13
14	15	16	17	18	19	20
21	22	23	24	25	26	27
28	29	30	31			

2023 **DECEMBER**

MONDAY
18

TODAY'S A GOOD DAY TO SEE THE LIGHT IN EVERYTHING.

TUESDAY
19

WEDNESDAY
20

TRADE YOUR FEAR OF THE UNKNOWN FOR THE FREEDOM TO THRIVE WITHIN IT.

THURSDAY
21

Winter begins (Northern Hemisphere)

FIND A NICE NOOK AND A REALLY GOOD BOOK.

FRIDAY 22

SATURDAY 23

SUNDAY 24

YOU'RE THE BEST PRESENT UNDER THAT TREE!

Christmas Eve

DON'T FORGET:

THIS WEEK'S HAPPY MOMENT:

DECEMBER 2023

S	M	T	W	T	F	S
					1	2
3	4	5	6	7	8	9
10	11	12	13	14	15	16
17	18	19	20	21	22	23
24/31	25	26	27	28	29	30

JANUARY 2024

S	M	T	W	T	F	S
	1	2	3	4	5	6
7	8	9	10	11	12	13
14	15	16	17	18	19	20
21	22	23	24	25	26	27
28	29	30	31			

2023 DECEMBER

MONDAY
25

Christmas Day

TUESDAY
26

YOU ARE *INHERENTLY* DESERVING
OF REST AND HAPPINESS.

Kwanzaa begins; Boxing Day (AUS, CAN, NZ, UK)

WEDNESDAY
27

THURSDAY
28

WHEN YOU FOCUS ON THE
GOOD, IT GETS BETTER.

FRIDAY
29

APPLAUD HOW MUCH YOU'VE DEVELOPED THIS YEAR!

SATURDAY
30

SUNDAY
31

New Year's Eve

DON'T FORGET:

DECEMBER 2023

S	M	T	W	T	F	S
					1	2
3	4	5	6	7	8	9
10	11	12	13	14	15	16
17	18	19	20	21	22	23
24/31	25	26	27	28	29	30

JANUARY 2024

S	M	T	W	T	F	S
	1	2	3	4	5	6
7	8	9	10	11	12	13
14	15	16	17	18	19	20
21	22	23	24	25	26	27
28	29	30	31			

THIS WEEK'S HAPPY MOMENT:

MONTHLY GOALS

NEW GOALS TO FOCUS ON

WHAT WORKED LAST MONTH

WHAT COULD BE BETTER

BE PROUD OF WHO YOU ARE

JANUARY 2024

SUNDAY	MONDAY	TUESDAY	WEDNESDAY	THURSDAY	FRIDAY	SATURDAY
31	1 New Year's Day	2 Day after New Year's Day (NZ, SCT)	3	4	5	6
7	8	9	10	11	12	13
14	15 Martin Luther King Jr. Day	16	17	18	19	20
21	22	23	24	25	26 Australia Day (AUS)	27
28	29	30	31	1	2	3

CREATURE OF HABIT

Track new goals or habits and watch your progress every month!

HABIT	1	2	3	4	5	6	7	8	9	10	11	12	13	14	15	16	17	18	19	20	21	22	23	24	25	26	27	28	29	30	31

2024 **JANUARY**

MONDAY
1

MAKE RESOLUTIONS? NAH. BUILD HABITS

New Year's Day

TUESDAY
2

Day after New Year's Day (NZ, SCT)

WEDNESDAY
3

DEAR FUTURE, *I AM READY.*

THURSDAY
4

THINGS MAY CHANGE, AND IT'S OK IF YOU DON'T CHANGE WITH THEM—OR IF YOU DO!

FRIDAY
5

SATURDAY
6

GOOD THINGS TAKE TIME.

SUNDAY
7

DON'T FORGET:

JANUARY 2024

S	M	T	W	T	F	S
	1	2	3	4	5	6
7	8	9	10	11	12	13
14	15	16	17	18	19	20
21	22	23	24	25	26	27
28	29	30	31			

FEBRUARY 2024

S	M	T	W	T	F	S
				1	2	3
4	5	6	7	8	9	10
11	12	13	14	15	16	17
18	19	20	21	22	23	24
25	26	27	28	29		

THIS WEEK'S HAPPY MOMENT:

2024 JANUARY

MONDAY
8

TUESDAY
9

WHAT ENERGIZES YOU? USE YOUR ANSWER TO JAZZ UP YOUR WEEK!

WEDNESDAY
10

THURSDAY
11

THE POWER OF POSITIVITY IS POSITIVELY ASTRONOMICAL!

FRIDAY
12

STARTING OVER IS JUST AN EXCITING NEW TRAIL TO EXPLORE.

SATURDAY
13

SUNDAY
14

DON'T FORGET:

THIS WEEK'S HAPPY MOMENT:

JANUARY 2024

S	M	T	W	T	F	S
	1	2	3	4	5	6
7	8	9	10	11	12	13
14	15	16	17	18	19	20
21	22	23	24	25	26	27
28	29	30	31			

FEBRUARY 2024

S	M	T	W	T	F	S
				1	2	3
4	5	6	7	8	9	10
11	12	13	14	15	16	17
18	19	20	21	22	23	24
25	26	27	28	29		

2024 JANUARY

MONDAY
15

DREAM FIERCELY!

Martin Luther King Jr. Day

TUESDAY
16

WEDNESDAY
17

YOU'RE THE UNDISPUTED WORLD
CHAMPION OF BEING *YOU*!

THURSDAY
18

STAY CURIOUS. THERE IS
ALWAYS MORE TO LEARN.

FRIDAY
19

SATURDAY
20

YOU DON'T JUST
ROCK, YOU ROLL!

SUNDAY
21

DON'T FORGET:

JANUARY 2024

S	M	T	W	T	F	S
	1	2	3	4	5	6
7	8	9	10	11	12	13
14	15	16	17	18	19	20
21	22	23	24	25	26	27
28	29	30	31			

FEBRUARY 2024

S	M	T	W	T	F	S
				1	2	3
4	5	6	7	8	9	10
11	12	13	14	15	16	17
18	19	20	21	22	23	24
25	26	27	28	29		

THIS WEEK'S
HAPPY MOMENT:

2024 **JANUARY**

MONDAY
22

TUESDAY
23

YOU'VE GOT A SMILE THAT CAN CHANGE WINTER TO SPRING!

WEDNESDAY
24

THURSDAY
25

JUST SAY "YIKES" AND MOVE ON!

FRIDAY 26

Australia Day (AUS)

CREATE THE LIFE YOU CAN'T WAIT TO WAKE UP TO.

SATURDAY 27

SUNDAY 28

DON'T FORGET:

THIS WEEK'S HAPPY MOMENT:

JANUARY 2024

S	M	T	W	T	F	S
	1	2	3	4	5	6
7	8	9	10	11	12	13
14	15	16	17	18	19	20
21	22	23	24	25	26	27
28	29	30	31			

FEBRUARY 2024

S	M	T	W	T	F	S
				1	2	3
4	5	6	7	8	9	10
11	12	13	14	15	16	17
18	19	20	21	22	23	24
25	26	27	28	29		

MONTHLY GOALS

NEW GOALS TO FOCUS ON

WHAT WORKED LAST MONTH

WHAT COULD BE BETTER

LOVE
YOUR
SELF

FEBRUARY 2024

SUNDAY	MONDAY	TUESDAY	WEDNESDAY	THURSDAY	FRIDAY	SATURDAY
28	29	30	31	1	2 Groundhog Day	3
4	5	6 Waitangi Day (NZ)	7	8	9	10 Chinese New Year
11	12 Abraham Lincoln's Birthday	13	14 Ash Wednesday (Lent begins); Valentine's Day	15	16	17
18	19 Presidents' Day	20	21	22	23	24
25	26	27	28	29	1	2

CREATURE OF HABIT

Track new goals or habits and watch your progress every month!

HABIT	1	2	3	4	5	6	7	8	9	10	11	12	13	14	15	16	17	18	19	20	21	22	23	24	25	26	27	28	29	30	31

2024 JANUARY/FEBRUARY

MONDAY
29

LOOKS LIKE A GOOD WEEK TO HAVE A GOOD WEEK.

TUESDAY
30

WEDNESDAY
31

KEEP GOING, KEEP GROWING.

THURSDAY
1

MANIFEST YOUR VISION.

FRIDAY
2

Groundhog Day

SATURDAY
3

LOVE *BIGGER.*
LIVE *BRIGHTER.*

SUNDAY
4

DON'T FORGET:

THIS WEEK'S
HAPPY MOMENT:

FEBRUARY 2024

S	M	T	W	T	F	S
				1	2	3
4	5	6	7	8	9	10
11	12	13	14	15	16	17
18	19	20	21	22	23	24
25	26	27	28	29		

MARCH 2024

S	M	T	W	T	F	S
					1	2
3	4	5	6	7	8	9
10	11	12	13	14	15	16
17	18	19	20	21	22	23
24/31	25	26	27	28	29	30

2024 **FEBRUARY**

MONDAY
5

TUESDAY
6

YOU CAN *DO THE THING.*

Waitangi Day (NZ)

WEDNESDAY
7

THURSDAY
8

PERFECT SHMERFECT.
CELEBRATE YOUR MISTAKES.

FRIDAY
9

YOU ARE CAPABLE OF GROWTH.

SATURDAY
10

Chinese New Year

SUNDAY
11

DON'T FORGET:

FEBRUARY 2024

S	M	T	W	T	F	S
				1	2	3
4	5	6	7	8	9	10
11	12	13	14	15	16	17
18	19	20	21	22	23	24
25	26	27	28	29		

MARCH 2024

S	M	T	W	T	F	S
					1	2
3	4	5	6	7	8	9
10	11	12	13	14	15	16
17	18	19	20	21	22	23
24/31	25	26	27	28	29	30

THIS WEEK'S HAPPY MOMENT:

2024 FEBRUARY

MONDAY
12

ASPIRE TO INSPIRE.

Abraham Lincoln's Birthday

TUESDAY
13

WEDNESDAY
14

TODAY'S SELF-CARE MENU:
H_2O, SWEATPANTS, CHOCOLATE.

Ash Wednesday (Lent begins); Valentine's Day

THURSDAY
15

SURROUND YOURSELF WITH PEOPLE
WHO INSPIRE YOU TO LIVE BOLDLY!

FRIDAY 16

SATURDAY 17

MAKE THE MOST OUT
OF THIS MOMENT!

SUNDAY 18

DON'T FORGET:

FEBRUARY 2024

S	M	T	W	T	F	S
				1	2	3
4	5	6	7	8	9	10
11	12	13	14	15	16	17
18	19	20	21	22	23	24
25	26	27	28	29		

MARCH 2024

S	M	T	W	T	F	S
					1	2
3	4	5	6	7	8	9
10	11	12	13	14	15	16
17	18	19	20	21	22	23
24/31	25	26	27	28	29	30

THIS WEEK'S
HAPPY MOMENT:

MONDAY
19

Presidents' Day

TUESDAY
20

IF YOU MAKE OTHERS HAPPY, YOUR OWN HAPPINESS MAY WORK ITSELF OUT.

WEDNESDAY
21

THURSDAY
22

SHOW OFF THAT INVINCIBLE SPIRIT! YOU'VE EARNED THE RIGHT TO BRAG.

FRIDAY
23

REMEMBER, NO ONE
HAS ALL THE ANSWERS.

SATURDAY
24

SUNDAY
25

DON'T FORGET:

FEBRUARY 2024

S	M	T	W	T	F	S
				1	2	3
4	5	6	7	8	9	10
11	12	13	14	15	16	17
18	19	20	21	22	23	24
25	26	27	28	29		

MARCH 2024

S	M	T	W	T	F	S
					1	2
3	4	5	6	7	8	9
10	11	12	13	14	15	16
17	18	19	20	21	22	23
24/31	25	26	27	28	29	30

THIS WEEK'S
HAPPY MOMENT:

MONDAY
26

NOTHING TURNS A BAD MOOD INTO A GOOD ONE LIKE CHOCOLATE.

TUESDAY
27

WEDNESDAY
28

THURSDAY
29

LEAP FOR JOY! WHAT WILL YOU DO WITH THE EXTRA DAY?

Leap Day

IN A WORLD WHERE YOU
CAN BE ANYTHING, BE KIND.

FRIDAY
1

SATURDAY
2

ALLOW YOURSELF SOME
DOWNTIME TO RESET.

SUNDAY
3

DON'T FORGET:

FEBRUARY 2024

S	M	T	W	T	F	S
				1	2	3
4	5	6	7	8	9	10
11	12	13	14	15	16	17
18	19	20	21	22	23	24
25	26	27	28	29		

MARCH 2024

S	M	T	W	T	F	S
					1	2
3	4	5	6	7	8	9
10	11	12	13	14	15	16
17	18	19	20	21	22	23
24/31	25	26	27	28	29	30

THIS WEEK'S
HAPPY MOMENT:

MONTHLY GOALS

NEW GOALS TO FOCUS ON

WHAT WORKED LAST MONTH

WHAT COULD BE BETTER

NEVER
SAY
NEVER

MARCH 2024

SUNDAY	MONDAY	TUESDAY	WEDNESDAY	THURSDAY	FRIDAY	SATURDAY
25	26	27	28	29	1	2
3	4	5	6	7	8 International Women's Day	9
10 Ramadan begins; Daylight Saving Time begins (USA, CAN); Mothering Sunday (UK)	11 Public Holiday (AUS: ACT, SA, TAS, VIC)	12	13	14	15	16
17 St. Patrick's Day	18	19 Spring begins (Northern Hemisphere)	20	21	22	23 Purim begins
24/31	25	26	27	28	29	30

CREATURE OF HABIT

Track new goals or habits and watch your progress every month!

HABIT	1	2	3	4	5	6	7	8	9	10	11	12	13	14	15	16	17	18	19	20	21	22	23	24	25	26	27	28	29	30	31

2024 **MARCH**

MONDAY
4

TUESDAY
5

IMPOSSIBLE LITERALLY SPELLS
"I'M POSSIBLE"!

WEDNESDAY
6

THURSDAY
7

EVERYTHING IS ITS OWN TEACHER, AND
THERE ARE ENDLESS THINGS TO LEARN.

FRIDAY
8

International Women's Day

LOOK IN THE MIRROR AND REMIND YOURSELF HOW BRILLIANT YOU ARE.

SATURDAY
9

SUNDAY
10

Ramadan begins; Daylight Saving Time begins (USA, CAN); Mothering Sunday (UK)

DON'T FORGET:

THIS WEEK'S HAPPY MOMENT:

MARCH 2024

S	M	T	W	T	F	S
					1	2
3	4	5	6	7	8	9
10	11	12	13	14	15	16
17	18	19	20	21	22	23
24/31	25	26	27	28	29	30

APRIL 2024

S	M	T	W	T	F	S
	1	2	3	4	5	6
7	8	9	10	11	12	13
14	15	16	17	18	19	20
21	22	23	24	25	26	27
28	29	30				

2024 MARCH

MONDAY
11

YOU DIDN'T LOSE AN HOUR. YOU'VE GOTTEN CLOSER TO YOUR DREAMS!

Public Holiday (AUS: ACT, SA, TAS, VIC)

TUESDAY
12

WEDNESDAY
13

HAVE YOU CONSIDERED THE WORLD IS LUCKY TO HAVE YOU?

THURSDAY
14

YOU'RE ON YOUR WAY TO
BIGGER AND BETTER THINGS.

FRIDAY 15

SATURDAY 16

YOU SHAMROCK
THE WORLD!

SUNDAY 17

St. Patrick's Day

DON'T FORGET:

MARCH 2024

S	M	T	W	T	F	S
					1	2
3	4	5	6	7	8	9
10	11	12	13	14	15	16
17	18	19	20	21	22	23
24/31	25	26	27	28	29	30

APRIL 2024

S	M	T	W	T	F	S
	1	2	3	4	5	6
7	8	9	10	11	12	13
14	15	16	17	18	19	20
21	22	23	24	25	26	27
28	29	30				

THIS WEEK'S
HAPPY MOMENT:

MONDAY
18

TUESDAY
19

TODAY'S FORECAST: SELF-LOVE SHOWERS AND SPRING FLOWERS!

Spring begins (Northern Hemisphere)

WEDNESDAY
20

THURSDAY
21

YOU'RE THE BEE'S KNEES.

FRIDAY
22

SAY "YES, I CAN"
ALL WEEKEND.

SATURDAY
23

Purim begins

SUNDAY
24

Palm Sunday

DON'T FORGET:

MARCH 2024

S	M	T	W	T	F	S
					1	2
3	4	5	6	7	8	9
10	11	12	13	14	15	16
17	18	19	20	21	22	23
24/31	25	26	27	28	29	30

APRIL 2024

S	M	T	W	T	F	S
	1	2	3	4	5	6
7	8	9	10	11	12	13
14	15	16	17	18	19	20
21	22	23	24	25	26	27
28	29	30				

THIS WEEK'S
HAPPY MOMENT:

2024 MARCH

MONDAY
25

IT'S OK TO NOT KNOW THE ANSWER, BUT DON'T BE AFRAID TO ASK THE QUESTION.

TUESDAY
26

WEDNESDAY
27

YOU'RE OUTTA THIS WORLD!

THURSDAY
28

PUT YOUR CHIN UP AND RISE!
IT'S A GOOD MORNING.

FRIDAY 29

Good Friday

SATURDAY 30

SUNDAY 31

IF YOU CAN'T FIND THE SUNSHINE, BE THE SUNSHINE.

Easter

DON'T FORGET:

MARCH 2024

S	M	T	W	T	F	S
					1	2
3	4	5	6	7	8	9
10	11	12	13	14	15	16
17	18	19	20	21	22	23
24/31	25	26	27	28	29	30

APRIL 2024

S	M	T	W	T	F	S
	1	2	3	4	5	6
7	8	9	10	11	12	13
14	15	16	17	18	19	20
21	22	23	24	25	26	27
28	29	30				

THIS WEEK'S HAPPY MOMENT:

MONTHLY GOALS

NEW GOALS TO FOCUS ON

WHAT WORKED LAST MONTH

WHAT COULD BE BETTER

YOUR
SPIRIT
is
ENDLESS

APRIL 2024

SUNDAY	MONDAY	TUESDAY	WEDNESDAY	THURSDAY	FRIDAY	SATURDAY
31	1 Easter Monday (AUS, CAN, NZ, UK except SCT); April Fools' Day	2	3	4	5	6
7	8	9 Eid al-Fitr begins	10	11	12	13
14	15 Tax Day	16	17	18	19	20
21	22 Passover begins; Earth Day	23	24	25 Anzac Day (AUS, NZ)	26	27
28 Workers' Memorial Day (UK)	29	30	1	2	3	4

CREATURE OF HABIT

Track new goals or habits and watch your progress every month!

HABIT	1	2	3	4	5	6	7	8	9	10	11	12	13	14	15	16	17	18	19	20	21	22	23	24	25	26	27	28	29	30	31

2024 APRIL

MONDAY
1

Easter Monday (AUS, CAN, NZ, UK except SCT); April Fools' Day

TUESDAY
2

NOTHING CAN RAIN ON YOUR PARADE TODAY!

WEDNESDAY
3

THURSDAY
4

A SETBACK JUST MEANS YOU'RE GETTING BETTER AT BEING YOU.

FRIDAY
5

YOU DESERVE TO
BE HAPPY. YOU
DESERVE DELIGHT.

SATURDAY
6

SUNDAY
7

DON'T FORGET:

APRIL 2024

S	M	T	W	T	F	S
	1	2	3	4	5	6
7	8	9	10	11	12	13
14	15	16	17	18	19	20
21	22	23	24	25	26	27
28	29	30				

MAY 2024

S	M	T	W	T	F	S
			1	2	3	4
5	6	7	8	9	10	11
12	13	14	15	16	17	18
19	20	21	22	23	24	25
26	27	28	29	30	31	

THIS WEEK'S
HAPPY MOMENT:

MONDAY
8

WRITE A MANTRA FOR YOUR WEEK AND REPEAT IT EACH MORNING.

TUESDAY
9

Eid al-Fitr begins

WEDNESDAY
10

NO GUTS, NO STORY.

THURSDAY
11

YOU GO AHEAD AND DO YOU.
YOU'RE A NATURAL AT IT.

FRIDAY
12

SATURDAY
13

NOTHING'S EVER TOO LATE, YOU'RE JUST ON YOUR OWN TIMELINE!

SUNDAY
14

DON'T FORGET:

APRIL 2024

S	M	T	W	T	F	S
	1	2	3	4	5	6
7	8	9	10	11	12	13
14	15	16	17	18	19	20
21	22	23	24	25	26	27
28	29	30				

MAY 2024

S	M	T	W	T	F	S
			1	2	3	4
5	6	7	8	9	10	11
12	13	14	15	16	17	18
19	20	21	22	23	24	25
26	27	28	29	30	31	

THIS WEEK'S HAPPY MOMENT:

2024 **APRIL**

MONDAY
15

Tax Day

TUESDAY
16

LIKE FLOWERS, YOU CAN'T THRIVE WITHOUT A LITTLE RAIN.

WEDNESDAY
17

THURSDAY
18

ANTI-BAD-MOOD SHIELD, *ACTIVATE*!

FRIDAY
19

INVENT A YOGA POSE
AND S-T-R-E-T-C-H.

SATURDAY
20

SUNDAY
21

DON'T FORGET:

APRIL 2024

S	M	T	W	T	F	S
	1	2	3	4	5	6
7	8	9	10	11	12	13
14	15	16	17	18	19	20
21	22	23	24	25	26	27
28	29	30				

MAY 2024

S	M	T	W	T	F	S
			1	2	3	4
5	6	7	8	9	10	11
12	13	14	15	16	17	18
19	20	21	22	23	24	25
26	27	28	29	30	31	

THIS WEEK'S
HAPPY MOMENT:

MONDAY
22

BE GENTLE WITH YOURSELF!
YOU'RE DOING THE BEST YOU CAN.

Passover begins; Earth Day

TUESDAY
23

WEDNESDAY
24

CELEBRATE EVERY SMALL WIN. YOU ROCK!

THURSDAY
25

Anzac Day (AUS, NZ)

MADE IT TO FRIYAY!

FRIDAY 26

SATURDAY 27

SUNDAY 28

YOU ARE 100% UNDISTILLED, PURE AMAZING!

Workers' Memorial Day (UK)

DON'T FORGET:

APRIL 2024

S	M	T	W	T	F	S
	1	2	3	4	5	6
7	8	9	10	11	12	13
14	15	16	17	18	19	20
21	22	23	24	25	26	27
28	29	30				

MAY 2024

S	M	T	W	T	F	S
			1	2	3	4
5	6	7	8	9	10	11
12	13	14	15	16	17	18
19	20	21	22	23	24	25
26	27	28	29	30	31	

THIS WEEK'S HAPPY MOMENT:

MONTHLY GOALS

NEW GOALS TO FOCUS ON

WHAT WORKED LAST MONTH

WHAT COULD BE BETTER

GOOD THINGS TAKE PLANNING
JUST BEGIN

MAY 2024

SUNDAY	MONDAY	TUESDAY	WEDNESDAY	THURSDAY	FRIDAY	SATURDAY
28	29	30	1	2	3	4
5 Cinco de Mayo	6	7	8	9	10	11
12 Mother's Day (USA, AUS, CAN, NZ)	13	14	15	16	17	18 Armed Forces Day
19	20 Victoria Day (CAN)	21	22	23	24	25
26	27 Memorial Day (USA); Spring Bank Holiday (UK)	28	29	30	31	1

CREATURE OF HABIT

Track new goals or habits and watch your progress every month!

HABIT	1	2	3	4	5	6	7	8	9	10	11	12	13	14	15	16	17	18	19	20	21	22	23	24	25	26	27	28	29	30	31

2024 **APRIL/MAY**

MONDAY
29

TUESDAY
30

FRESH AIR IS THE BEST CURE
FOR A LONG WEEK.

WEDNESDAY
1

THURSDAY
2

YOU'RE STRONGER EVERY DAY.

FRIDAY
3

YOU CAN'T STOP THE WAVES, BUT YOU CAN LEARN TO SURF.

SATURDAY
4

SUNDAY
5

Cinco de Mayo

DON'T FORGET:

THIS WEEK'S HAPPY MOMENT:

MAY 2024

S	M	T	W	T	F	S
			1	2	3	4
5	6	7	8	9	10	11
12	13	14	15	16	17	18
19	20	21	22	23	24	25
26	27	28	29	30	31	

JUNE 2024

S	M	T	W	T	F	S
						1
2	3	4	5	6	7	8
9	10	11	12	13	14	15
16	17	18	19	20	21	22
23/30	24	25	26	27	28	29

2024 **MAY**

MONDAY
6

KNOW WHAT YOU WANT, AND DON'T BE AFRAID TO GO OUT AND GET IT.

TUESDAY
7

WEDNESDAY
8

BE YOUR OWN BIGGEST FAN!

THURSDAY
9

LOOKS LIKE A COLOR-OUTSIDE-THE-LINES TYPE OF DAY!

FRIDAY 10

SATURDAY 11

YOU ARE POSITIVELY *DAZZLING*.

SUNDAY 12

Mother's Day (USA, AUS, CAN, NZ)

DON'T FORGET:

MAY 2024

S	M	T	W	T	F	S
			1	2	3	4
5	6	7	8	9	10	11
12	13	14	15	16	17	18
19	20	21	22	23	24	25
26	27	28	29	30	31	

JUNE 2024

S	M	T	W	T	F	S
						1
2	3	4	5	6	7	8
9	10	11	12	13	14	15
16	17	18	19	20	21	22
23/30	24	25	26	27	28	29

THIS WEEK'S HAPPY MOMENT:

2024 MAY

MONDAY
13

TUESDAY
14

TODAY'S MISSION: MAKE SOMEONE FEEL GOOD ABOUT THEMSELVES.

WEDNESDAY
15

THURSDAY
16

BE THE TYPE OF PERSON YOU WANT TO MEET.

FRIDAY
17

STRENGTHEN YOUR BOUNDARIES. "*NO*" IS A POWERFUL WORD.

SATURDAY
18

Armed Forces Day

SUNDAY
19

DON'T FORGET:

MAY 2024

S	M	T	W	T	F	S
			1	2	3	4
5	6	7	8	9	10	11
12	13	14	15	16	17	18
19	20	21	22	23	24	25
26	27	28	29	30	31	

JUNE 2024

S	M	T	W	T	F	S
						1
2	3	4	5	6	7	8
9	10	11	12	13	14	15
16	17	18	19	20	21	22
23/30	24	25	26	27	28	29

THIS WEEK'S HAPPY MOMENT:

MONDAY
20

WHERE DO YOU LIKE TO BE IN NATURE?
IF YOU CAN, GO THERE THIS WEEK!

Victoria Day (CAN)

TUESDAY
21

WEDNESDAY
22

TRUST IN YOU. YOU WILL NEVER
LEAVE YOURSELF BEHIND.

THURSDAY
23

YOU DO NOT HAVE TO BE PRODUCTIVE TO HAVE VALUE. ALLOW YOURSELF TIME TO JUST BE.

FRIDAY 24

SATURDAY 25

SUNDAY 26

HOME'S NOT A PLACE, IT'S A FEELING.

DON'T FORGET:

MAY 2024

S	M	T	W	T	F	S
			1	2	3	4
5	6	7	8	9	10	11
12	13	14	15	16	17	18
19	20	21	22	23	24	25
26	27	28	29	30	31	

JUNE 2024

S	M	T	W	T	F	S
						1
2	3	4	5	6	7	8
9	10	11	12	13	14	15
16	17	18	19	20	21	22
23/30	24	25	26	27	28	29

THIS WEEK'S HAPPY MOMENT:

MONDAY
27

Memorial Day (USA); Spring Bank Holiday (UK)

TUESDAY
28

IT'S ALL COMING TOGETHER.

WEDNESDAY
29

THURSDAY
30

SOMETIMES YOU'VE GOTTA CLIMB
A MOUNTAIN OF NO'S FOR THAT YES

FRIDAY
31

THE BEST THING YOU CAN BE IS *YOU*.

SATURDAY
1

SUNDAY
2

DON'T FORGET:

MAY 2024

S	M	T	W	T	F	S
			1	2	3	4
5	6	7	8	9	10	11
12	13	14	15	16	17	18
19	20	21	22	23	24	25
26	27	28	29	30	31	

JUNE 2024

S	M	T	W	T	F	S
						1
2	3	4	5	6	7	8
9	10	11	12	13	14	15
16	17	18	19	20	21	22
23/30	24	25	26	27	28	29

THIS WEEK'S HAPPY MOMENT:

MONTHLY GOALS

NEW GOALS TO FOCUS ON

WHAT WORKED LAST MONTH

WHAT COULD BE BETTER

Let
your Soul
SHINE

JUNE 2024

SUNDAY	MONDAY	TUESDAY	WEDNESDAY	THURSDAY	FRIDAY	SATURDAY
26	27	28	29	30	31	1
2	3	4	5	6	7	8
9	10	11 Shavuot begins	12	13	14 Flag Day	15
16 Eid al-Adha begins; Father's Day (USA, CAN, UK)	17	18	19 Juneteenth	20 Summer begins (Northern Hemisphere)	21	22
23/30	24	25	26	27	28	29

CREATURE OF HABIT

Track new goals or habits and watch your progress every month!

HABIT	1	2	3	4	5	6	7	8	9	10	11	12	13	14	15	16	17	18	19	20	21	22	23	24	25	26	27	28	29	30	31

2024 JUNE

MONDAY
3

SUNSHINE IS HERE! GO FEEL THE GRASS BETWEEN YOUR TOES.

TUESDAY
4

WEDNESDAY
5

DON'T LET ONE BUMP IN THE ROAD KEEP YOU FROM MOVING FORWARD.

THURSDAY
6

ROLL DOWN THE WINDOWS.
CRANK UP THE MUSIC. SING!

FRIDAY 7

SATURDAY 8

SUNDAY 9

EVERY DAY IS A
SPECIAL OCCASION!

DON'T FORGET:

THIS WEEK'S
HAPPY MOMENT:

JUNE 2024

S	M	T	W	T	F	S
						1
2	3	4	5	6	7	8
9	10	11	12	13	14	15
16	17	18	19	20	21	22
23/30	24	25	26	27	28	29

JULY 2024

S	M	T	W	T	F	S
	1	2	3	4	5	6
7	8	9	10	11	12	13
14	15	16	17	18	19	20
21	22	23	24	25	26	27
28	29	30	31			

2024 JUNE

MONDAY
10

TUESDAY
11

INHALE. EXHALE. ALL IS WELL.

Shavuot begins

WEDNESDAY
12

THURSDAY
13

HAPPINESS IS NOT A STATE TO ARRIVE AT BUT A MANNER OF TRAVELING.

FRIDAY
14

Flag Day

BE NORMAL? PAH!
YOU'RE TOO MUCH FUN!

SATURDAY
15

SUNDAY
16

Eid al-Adha begins; Father's Day (USA, CAN, UK)

DON'T FORGET:

JUNE 2024

S	M	T	W	T	F	S
						1
2	3	4	5	6	7	8
9	10	11	12	13	14	15
16	17	18	19	20	21	22
23/30	24	25	26	27	28	29

JULY 2024

S	M	T	W	T	F	S
	1	2	3	4	5	6
7	8	9	10	11	12	13
14	15	16	17	18	19	20
21	22	23	24	25	26	27
28	29	30	31			

THIS WEEK'S
HAPPY MOMENT:

MONDAY
17

WAKE UP. CONQUER THE WORLD. REPEAT.

TUESDAY
18

WEDNESDAY
19

MAGIC'S NOT REAL? SAYS WHO?

Juneteenth

THURSDAY
20

Summer begins (Northern Hemisphere)

TIME FOR A SUPER-DUPER SUMMER!

FRIDAY
21

SATURDAY
22

EASY-PEASY
LEMON SQUEEZY!

SUNDAY
23

DON'T FORGET:

JUNE 2024

S	M	T	W	T	F	S
						1
2	3	4	5	6	7	8
9	10	11	12	13	14	15
16	17	18	19	20	21	22
23/30	24	25	26	27	28	29

JULY 2024

S	M	T	W	T	F	S
	1	2	3	4	5	6
7	8	9	10	11	12	13
14	15	16	17	18	19	20
21	22	23	24	25	26	27
28	29	30	31			

THIS WEEK'S
HAPPY MOMENT:

2024 JUNE

MONDAY
24

TUESDAY
25

GETTING LOST MAY BE THE
WAY TO FIND YOURSELF.

WEDNESDAY
26

THURSDAY
27

TAKE A DEEP BREATH.
BLOW OUT YESTERDAY'S TROUBLES.

FRIDAY
28

LOVE IS LOVE IS LOVE
IS LOVE IS LOVE IS
LOVE IS LOVE IS LOVE
IS LOVE IS LOVE.

SATURDAY
29

SUNDAY
30

DON'T FORGET:

JUNE 2024

S	M	T	W	T	F	S
						1
2	3	4	5	6	7	8
9	10	11	12	13	14	15
16	17	18	19	20	21	22
23/30	24	25	26	27	28	29

JULY 2024

S	M	T	W	T	F	S
	1	2	3	4	5	6
7	8	9	10	11	12	13
14	15	16	17	18	19	20
21	22	23	24	25	26	27
28	29	30	31			

THIS WEEK'S
HAPPY MOMENT:

MONTHLY GOALS

NEW GOALS TO FOCUS ON

WHAT WORKED LAST MONTH

WHAT COULD BE BETTER

YOU ARE A STAR AMONGST COMETS!

JULY 2024

SUNDAY	MONDAY	TUESDAY	WEDNESDAY	THURSDAY	FRIDAY	SATURDAY
30	1 Canada Day (CAN)	2	3	4 Independence Day	5	6
7	8	9	10	11	12 Orangemen's Day— Battle of the Boyne (NIR)	13
14	15	16	17	18	19	20
21	22	23	24	25	26	27
28	29	30	31	1	2	3

CREATURE OF HABIT

Track new goals or habits and watch your progress every month!

HABIT	1	2	3	4	5	6	7	8	9	10	11	12	13	14	15	16	17	18	19	20	21	22	23	24	25	26	27	28	29	30	31

MONDAY
1

DO YOU KNOW HOW RADIANT YOU ARE?

Canada Day (CAN)

TUESDAY
2

WEDNESDAY
3

BE YOUR OWN KIND OF BEAUTIFUL.

THURSDAY
4

Independence Day

LIGHT UP YOUR DAY LIKE FIREWORKS!

FRIDAY
5

SATURDAY
6

WHEN IN DOUBT, BUY MORE PLANTS!

SUNDAY
7

DON'T FORGET:

JULY 2024

S	M	T	W	T	F	S
	1	2	3	4	5	6
7	8	9	10	11	12	13
14	15	16	17	18	19	20
21	22	23	24	25	26	27
28	29	30	31			

AUGUST 2024

S	M	T	W	T	F	S
				1	2	3
4	5	6	7	8	9	10
11	12	13	14	15	16	17
18	19	20	21	22	23	24
25	26	27	28	29	30	31

THIS WEEK'S HAPPY MOMENT:

MONDAY
8

TUESDAY
9

HOPE FLOATS, AND GROWS, AND FLOWS. THERE'S ALWAYS ROOM FOR MORE.

WEDNESDAY
10

THURSDAY
11

INGREDIENTS FOR A GOOD DAY: SUN, FUN, AND *YOU*!

FRIDAY
12

Orangemen's Day—Battle of the Boyne (NIR)

CTRL + ALT + DELETE
NEGATIVITY

SATURDAY
13

SUNDAY
14

DON'T FORGET:

JULY 2024

S	M	T	W	T	F	S
	1	2	3	4	5	6
7	8	9	10	11	12	13
14	15	16	17	18	19	20
21	22	23	24	25	26	27
28	29	30	31			

AUGUST 2024

S	M	T	W	T	F	S
				1	2	3
4	5	6	7	8	9	10
11	12	13	14	15	16	17
18	19	20	21	22	23	24
25	26	27	28	29	30	31

THIS WEEK'S
HAPPY MOMENT:

2024 JULY

MONDAY
15

WHERE IS YOUR HAPPY PLACE? GET OVER THERE FOR AN AFTERNOON PICK-ME-UP

TUESDAY
16

WEDNESDAY
17

CONFIDENCE CHANGES EVERYTHING.

THURSDAY
18

FIND OTHERS WHO CAN MATCH YOUR WEIRD.

FRIDAY
19

SATURDAY
20

THE WORLD IS A BETTER PLACE WITH YOU IN IT.

SUNDAY
21

DON'T FORGET:

THIS WEEK'S HAPPY MOMENT:

JULY 2024

S	M	T	W	T	F	S
	1	2	3	4	5	6
7	8	9	10	11	12	13
14	15	16	17	18	19	20
21	22	23	24	25	26	27
28	29	30	31			

AUGUST 2024

S	M	T	W	T	F	S
				1	2	3
4	5	6	7	8	9	10
11	12	13	14	15	16	17
18	19	20	21	22	23	24
25	26	27	28	29	30	31

2024 JULY

MONDAY
22

TUESDAY
23

YOU DON'T HAVE TO BE SURE
HOW, JUST THAT YOU WILL.

WEDNESDAY
24

THURSDAY
25

SLOW DOWN AND SOAK UP THE SUNSHINE.

FRIDAY
26

HOW DID YOU TAKE CARE OF YOURSELF THIS WEEK?

SATURDAY
27

SUNDAY
28

DON'T FORGET:

JULY 2024

S	M	T	W	T	F	S
	1	2	3	4	5	6
7	8	9	10	11	12	13
14	15	16	17	18	19	20
21	22	23	24	25	26	27
28	29	30	31			

AUGUST 2024

S	M	T	W	T	F	S
				1	2	3
4	5	6	7	8	9	10
11	12	13	14	15	16	17
18	19	20	21	22	23	24
25	26	27	28	29	30	31

THIS WEEK'S HAPPY MOMENT:

MONTHLY GOALS

NEW GOALS TO FOCUS ON

WHAT WORKED LAST MONTH

WHAT COULD BE BETTER

YOU'RE
more than
enough

AUGUST 2024

SUNDAY	MONDAY	TUESDAY	WEDNESDAY	THURSDAY	FRIDAY	SATURDAY
28	29	30	31	1	2	3
4	5 Summer Bank Holiday (SCT)	6	7	8	9	10
11	12	13	14	15	16	17
18	19	20	21	22	23	24
25	26 Summer Bank Holiday (UK except SCT)	27	28	29	30	31

CREATURE OF HABIT

Track new goals or habits and watch your progress every month!

HABIT	1	2	3	4	5	6	7	8	9	10	11	12	13	14	15	16	17	18	19	20	21	22	23	24	25	26	27	28	29	30	31

MONDAY
29

BELIEVE IN SOMETHING NEW.

TUESDAY
30

WEDNESDAY
31

THE SUN GOT UP EARLY TO SEE *YOU*.

THURSDAY
1

WELCOME A WELLNESS DAY. GO OUTSIDE AND BOOST YOUR SPIRITS!

FRIDAY
2

SATURDAY
3

DON'T WORRY. CHOOSE HAPPY.

SUNDAY
4

DON'T FORGET:

AUGUST 2024

S	M	T	W	T	F	S
				1	2	3
4	5	6	7	8	9	10
11	12	13	14	15	16	17
18	19	20	21	22	23	24
25	26	27	28	29	30	31

SEPTEMBER 2024

S	M	T	W	T	F	S
1	2	3	4	5	6	7
8	9	10	11	12	13	14
15	16	17	18	19	20	21
22	23	24	25	26	27	28
29	30					

THIS WEEK'S HAPPY MOMENT:

2024 AUGUST

MONDAY
5

Summer Bank Holiday (SCT)

TUESDAY
6

THERE IS NO ANGRY WAY TO SAY THE WORD ***BUBBLES***. TRY IT!

WEDNESDAY
7

THURSDAY
8

THE WORLD IS YOUR OYSTER. WHAT FANTASTIC THING CAN YOU DO NEXT?

FRIDAY
9

SUNSHINE MAKES YOU HAPPIER. SOAK UP THOSE RAYS THIS WEEKEND!

SATURDAY
10

SUNDAY
11

DON'T FORGET:

AUGUST 2024

S	M	T	W	T	F	S
				1	2	3
4	5	6	7	8	9	10
11	12	13	14	15	16	17
18	19	20	21	22	23	24
25	26	27	28	29	30	31

SEPTEMBER 2024

S	M	T	W	T	F	S
1	2	3	4	5	6	7
8	9	10	11	12	13	14
15	16	17	18	19	20	21
22	23	24	25	26	27	28
29	30					

THIS WEEK'S HAPPY MOMENT:

MONDAY
12

LIKE FLECKS OF GOLD, EVERY NEW EXPERIENCE MAKES YOU RICHER.

TUESDAY
13

WEDNESDAY
14

THERE IS AN INNER CHILD IN ALL OF US. DO SOMETHING SILLY TODAY!

THURSDAY
15

LOST YOUR TO-DO LIST? EXCELLENT!

FRIDAY 16

SATURDAY 17

A HOT DAY BUT A SERIOUSLY COOL *YOU*.

SUNDAY 18

DON'T FORGET:

AUGUST 2024

S	M	T	W	T	F	S
				1	2	3
4	5	6	7	8	9	10
11	12	13	14	15	16	17
18	19	20	21	22	23	24
25	26	27	28	29	30	31

SEPTEMBER 2024

S	M	T	W	T	F	S
1	2	3	4	5	6	7
8	9	10	11	12	13	14
15	16	17	18	19	20	21
22	23	24	25	26	27	28
29	30					

THIS WEEK'S HAPPY MOMENT:

2024 **AUGUST**

MONDAY
19

TUESDAY
20

MAKE LIKE A FLOWER AND BLOOM.

WEDNESDAY
21

THURSDAY
22

WELCOME TO AFFIRMATION STATION! YOU ARE WONDERFUL.

FRIDAY
23

LIKE A MERMAID,
YOU MAKE WAVES.

SATURDAY
24

SUNDAY
25

DON'T FORGET:

AUGUST 2024

S	M	T	W	T	F	S
				1	2	3
4	5	6	7	8	9	10
11	12	13	14	15	16	17
18	19	20	21	22	23	24
25	26	27	28	29	30	31

SEPTEMBER 2024

S	M	T	W	T	F	S
1	2	3	4	5	6	7
8	9	10	11	12	13	14
15	16	17	18	19	20	21
22	23	24	25	26	27	28
29	30					

THIS WEEK'S
HAPPY MOMENT:

MONDAY
26

BE PROUD OF WHO YOU ARE.

Summer Bank Holiday (UK except SCT)

TUESDAY
27

WEDNESDAY
28

THINK IT, WANT IT, GET IT!

THURSDAY
29

DOODLE SOMETHING THAT DELIGHTS YOU AND HANG IT WHERE YOU CAN SEE IT.

FRIDAY
30

SATURDAY
31

WHAT COULD YOU DO TODAY THAT YOU WILL REMEMBER FOREVER?

SUNDAY
1

Father's Day (AUS, NZ)

DON'T FORGET:

AUGUST 2024

S	M	T	W	T	F	S
				1	2	3
4	5	6	7	8	9	10
11	12	13	14	15	16	17
18	19	20	21	22	23	24
25	26	27	28	29	30	31

SEPTEMBER 2024

S	M	T	W	T	F	S
1	2	3	4	5	6	7
8	9	10	11	12	13	14
15	16	17	18	19	20	21
22	23	24	25	26	27	28
29	30					

THIS WEEK'S HAPPY MOMENT:

MONTHLY GOALS

NEW GOALS TO FOCUS ON

WHAT WORKED LAST MONTH

WHAT COULD BE BETTER

It's
OKAY to
have
bad days

SEPTEMBER 2024

SUNDAY	MONDAY	TUESDAY	WEDNESDAY	THURSDAY	FRIDAY	SATURDAY
1 Father's Day (AUS, NZ)	2 Labor Day (USA, CAN)	3	4	5	6	7
8	9	10	11 Patriot Day	12	13	14
15	16	17	18	19	20	21
22 Autumn begins (Northern Hemisphere)	23	24	25	26	27	28
29	30	1	2	3	4	5

CREATURE OF HABIT

Track new goals or habits and watch your progress every month!

HABIT	1	2	3	4	5	6	7	8	9	10	11	12	13	14	15	16	17	18	19	20	21	22	23	24	25	26	27	28	29	30	31

2024 SEPTEMBER

MONDAY
2

Labor Day (USA, CAN)

TUESDAY
3

YOU'RE ONE TOUGH COOKIE.

WEDNESDAY
4

THURSDAY
5

TIME FOR A MENTAL VACATION.

FRIDAY
6

WEAR YOUR
CONFIDENCE CROWN
ALL WEEKEND LONG.

SATURDAY
7

SUNDAY
8

DON'T FORGET:

SEPTEMBER 2024

S	M	T	W	T	F	S
1	2	3	4	5	6	7
8	9	10	11	12	13	14
15	16	17	18	19	20	21
22	23	24	25	26	27	28
29	30					

OCTOBER 2024

S	M	T	W	T	F	S
		1	2	3	4	5
6	7	8	9	10	11	12
13	14	15	16	17	18	19
20	21	22	23	24	25	26
27	28	29	30	31		

THIS WEEK'S
HAPPY MOMENT:

2024 **SEPTEMBER**

MONDAY
9

IT DOES NOT MAKE YOU IRRESPONSIBLE IF EVERYTHING IN YOUR LIFE HAS NOT YET BEEN PLANNED.

TUESDAY
10

WEDNESDAY
11

THERE IS NO RIGHT WAY TO FEEL RIGHT NOW.

Patriot Day

THURSDAY
12

SMILE SO BRIGHT YOU HAVE TO WEAR SHADES!

FRIDAY 13

SATURDAY 14

SUNDAY 15

YOU DESERVE A MINI ADVENTURE! TAKE A FIVE-MINUTE STROLL TODAY.

DON'T FORGET:

SEPTEMBER 2024

S	M	T	W	T	F	S
1	2	3	4	5	6	7
8	9	10	11	12	13	14
15	16	17	18	19	20	21
22	23	24	25	26	27	28
29	30					

OCTOBER 2024

S	M	T	W	T	F	S
		1	2	3	4	5
6	7	8	9	10	11	12
13	14	15	16	17	18	19
20	21	22	23	24	25	26
27	28	29	30	31		

THIS WEEK'S HAPPY MOMENT:

2024 **SEPTEMBER**

MONDAY
16

TUESDAY
17

GO TO BED EARLY TONIGHT. YOUR BODY WILL THANK YOU IN THE MORNING!

WEDNESDAY
18

THURSDAY
19

TODAY IS CLOUDY WITH A CHANCE OF ***AWESOME.***

FRIDAY 20

YOUR AMAZING-O-METER IS WAY OFF THE CHARTS!

SATURDAY 21

SUNDAY 22

Autumn begins (Northern Hemisphere)

DON'T FORGET:

SEPTEMBER 2024

S	M	T	W	T	F	S
1	2	3	4	5	6	7
8	9	10	11	12	13	14
15	16	17	18	19	20	21
22	23	24	25	26	27	28
29	30					

OCTOBER 2024

S	M	T	W	T	F	S
		1	2	3	4	5
6	7	8	9	10	11	12
13	14	15	16	17	18	19
20	21	22	23	24	25	26
27	28	29	30	31		

THIS WEEK'S HAPPY MOMENT:

2024 **SEPTEMBER**

MONDAY
23

WHY BE REGULAR WHEN YOU CAN BE **BOLD** OR *ITALIC*?

TUESDAY
24

WEDNESDAY
25

CAREFREE, NOT CARELESS.

THURSDAY
26

YOU CAN *ALWAYS* TRY AGAIN.

FRIDAY 27

SATURDAY 28

SHOW YOURSELF MORE LOVE.

SUNDAY 29

DON'T FORGET:

SEPTEMBER 2024

S	M	T	W	T	F	S
1	2	3	4	5	6	7
8	9	10	11	12	13	14
15	16	17	18	19	20	21
22	23	24	25	26	27	28
29	30					

OCTOBER 2024

S	M	T	W	T	F	S
		1	2	3	4	5
6	7	8	9	10	11	12
13	14	15	16	17	18	19
20	21	22	23	24	25	26
27	28	29	30	31		

THIS WEEK'S HAPPY MOMENT:

MONTHLY GOALS

NEW GOALS TO FOCUS ON

WHAT WORKED LAST MONTH

WHAT COULD BE BETTER

Be the
Magic
not the
Illusion

OCTOBER 2024

SUNDAY	MONDAY	TUESDAY	WEDNESDAY	THURSDAY	FRIDAY	SATURDAY
29	30	1	2 Rosh Hashanah begins	3	4	5
6	7	8	9	10	11 Yom Kippur begins	12
13	14 Columbus Day (USA); Indigenous Peoples' Day (USA); Thanksgiving Day (CAN)	15	16 Sukkot begins	17	18	19
20	21	22	23	24	25	26
27	28	29	30	31 Diwali begins; Halloween	1	2

CREATURE OF HABIT

Track new goals or habits and watch your progress every month!

HABIT	1	2	3	4	5	6	7	8	9	10	11	12	13	14	15	16	17	18	19	20	21	22	23	24	25	26	27	28	29	30	31

2024 SEPTEMBER/OCTOBER

MONDAY
30

TUESDAY
1

YOU MAY NOT ALWAYS FEEL LIKE THE STAR YOU ARE, BUT YOU KEEP SHINING ANYWAY!

WEDNESDAY
2

Rosh Hashanah begins

THURSDAY
3

HAPPY FRIDAY EVE!

FRIDAY
4

YOU ARE MORE THAN
GOOD ENOUGH.

SATURDAY
5

SUNDAY
6

DON'T FORGET:

OCTOBER 2024

S	M	T	W	T	F	S
		1	2	3	4	5
6	7	8	9	10	11	12
13	14	15	16	17	18	19
20	21	22	23	24	25	26
27	28	29	30	31		

NOVEMBER 2024

S	M	T	W	T	F	S
					1	2
3	4	5	6	7	8	9
10	11	12	13	14	15	16
17	18	19	20	21	22	23
24	25	26	27	28	29	30

THIS WEEK'S
HAPPY MOMENT:

2024 OCTOBER

MONDAY
7

WORDS ARE POWERFUL. USE THEM TOWARD YOURSELF AND OTHERS WISELY.

TUESDAY
8

WEDNESDAY
9

YOU CAN WEATHER ANY STORM.

THURSDAY
10

TELL A FRIEND WHY YOU LOVE THEM!
EVERYONE DESERVES TO KNOW
WHAT MAKES THEM SPECIAL.

FRIDAY
11

Yom Kippur begins

SATURDAY
12

DON'T WAIT. CHASE
WHAT YOU WANT.

SUNDAY
13

DON'T FORGET:

OCTOBER 2024

S	M	T	W	T	F	S
		1	2	3	4	5
6	7	8	9	10	11	12
13	14	15	16	17	18	19
20	21	22	23	24	25	26
27	28	29	30	31		

NOVEMBER 2024

S	M	T	W	T	F	S
					1	2
3	4	5	6	7	8	9
10	11	12	13	14	15	16
17	18	19	20	21	22	23
24	25	26	27	28	29	30

THIS WEEK'S
HAPPY MOMENT:

2024 OCTOBER

MONDAY
14

Columbus Day (USA); Indigenous Peoples' Day (USA); Thanksgiving Day (CAN)

TUESDAY
15

PROTECT YOUR PEACE.

WEDNESDAY
16

Sukkot begins

THURSDAY
17

YOU'RE ALLOWED TO DO THINGS DIFFERENTLY.

FRIDAY
18

LEARN TO REST,
NOT TO QUIT.

SATURDAY
19

SUNDAY
20

DON'T FORGET:

OCTOBER 2024

S	M	T	W	T	F	S
		1	2	3	4	5
6	7	8	9	10	11	12
13	14	15	16	17	18	19
20	21	22	23	24	25	26
27	28	29	30	31		

NOVEMBER 2024

S	M	T	W	T	F	S
					1	2
3	4	5	6	7	8	9
10	11	12	13	14	15	16
17	18	19	20	21	22	23
24	25	26	27	28	29	30

THIS WEEK'S
HAPPY MOMENT:

2024 **OCTOBER**

MONDAY
21

LET IT BE KNOWN THAT THE UNKNOWN DOESN'T INTIMIDATE YOU.

TUESDAY
22

WEDNESDAY
23

YOU'RE A WHOLE LOT OF LOVELY!

THURSDAY
24

EVEN THE DARKEST CLOUDS
HAVE SILVER LININGS.

FRIDAY
25

SATURDAY
26

SUNDAY
27

IT'S TAKE-A-CHANCE WEEKEND. ROLL THE DICE AND TRY SOMETHING NEW!

DON'T FORGET:

OCTOBER 2024

S	M	T	W	T	F	S
		1	2	3	4	5
6	7	8	9	10	11	12
13	14	15	16	17	18	19
20	21	22	23	24	25	26
27	28	29	30	31		

NOVEMBER 2024

S	M	T	W	T	F	S
					1	2
3	4	5	6	7	8	9
10	11	12	13	14	15	16
17	18	19	20	21	22	23
24	25	26	27	28	29	30

THIS WEEK'S
HAPPY MOMENT:

MONDAY
28

TUESDAY
29

YOU ARE MORE CAPABLE THAN YOU REALIZE.

WEDNESDAY
30

THURSDAY
31

HOLD ON TO YOUR WONDER.

Diwali begins; Halloween

FRIDAY
1

SATURDAY
2

LOOK AT THAT—AN EXTRA HOUR TO BE MARVELOUS COMING UP!

SUNDAY
3

Daylight Saving Time ends (USA, CAN)

DON'T FORGET:

OCTOBER 2024

S	M	T	W	T	F	S
		1	2	3	4	5
6	7	8	9	10	11	12
13	14	15	16	17	18	19
20	21	22	23	24	25	26
27	28	29	30	31		

NOVEMBER 2024

S	M	T	W	T	F	S
					1	2
3	4	5	6	7	8	9
10	11	12	13	14	15	16
17	18	19	20	21	22	23
24	25	26	27	28	29	30

THIS WEEK'S HAPPY MOMENT:

MONTHLY GOALS

NEW GOALS TO FOCUS ON

WHAT WORKED LAST MONTH

WHAT COULD BE BETTER

some things are worth waiting for

NOVEMBER 2024

SUNDAY	MONDAY	TUESDAY	WEDNESDAY	THURSDAY	FRIDAY	SATURDAY
27	28	29	30	31	1	2
3 Daylight Saving Time ends (USA, CAN)	4	5 Election Day	6	7	8	9
10	11 Veterans Day (USA); Remembrance Day (CAN, UK)	12	13	14	15	16
17	18	19	20	21	22	23
24	25	26	27	28	29	30

CREATURE OF HABIT

Track new goals or habits and watch your progress every month!

HABIT	1	2	3	4	5	6	7	8	9	10	11	12	13	14	15	16	17	18	19	20	21	22	23	24	25	26	27	28	29	30	31

MONDAY
4

RECLAIM YOUR HAPPINESS.

TUESDAY
5

Election Day

WEDNESDAY
6

YOU ARE THE BEST INVESTMENT
YOU'LL EVER MAKE.

THURSDAY
7

GO FOR IT! DON'T OVERTHINK.

FRIDAY
8

SATURDAY
9

IT'S OK TO NOT DO EVERYTHING.

SUNDAY
10

DON'T FORGET:

NOVEMBER 2024

S	M	T	W	T	F	S
					1	2
3	4	5	6	7	8	9
10	11	12	13	14	15	16
17	18	19	20	21	22	23
24	25	26	27	28	29	30

DECEMBER 2024

S	M	T	W	T	F	S
1	2	3	4	5	6	7
8	9	10	11	12	13	14
15	16	17	18	19	20	21
22	23	24	25	26	27	28
29	30	31				

THIS WEEK'S HAPPY MOMENT:

2024 NOVEMBER

MONDAY
11

Veterans Day (USA); Remembrance Day (CAN, UK)

TUESDAY
12

PRACTICE MAKES PROGRESS.

WEDNESDAY
13

THURSDAY
14

DON'T BE AFRAID TO FOLLOW
YOUR OWN ROADMAP.

FRIDAY
15

SATURDAY
16

MAKE IT A NO-INTERRUPTIONS DAY! WHAT WILL YOU DO WITH THE QUIET?

SUNDAY
17

DON'T FORGET:

NOVEMBER 2024

S	M	T	W	T	F	S
					1	2
3	4	5	6	7	8	9
10	11	12	13	14	15	16
17	18	19	20	21	22	23
24	25	26	27	28	29	30

DECEMBER 2024

S	M	T	W	T	F	S
1	2	3	4	5	6	7
8	9	10	11	12	13	14
15	16	17	18	19	20	21
22	23	24	25	26	27	28
29	30	31				

THIS WEEK'S HAPPY MOMENT:

MONDAY
18

COMEBACKS ARE STRONGER
THAN SETBACKS.

TUESDAY
19

WEDNESDAY
20

DROP THE SELF-PRESSURE.
PICK UP MORE PATIENCE.

THURSDAY
21

DO MORE WORK THAT FEELS LIKE PLAY.

FRIDAY
22

SATURDAY
23

TOUGH TIMES
NEVER LAST.

SUNDAY
24

DON'T FORGET:

NOVEMBER 2024

S	M	T	W	T	F	S
					1	2
3	4	5	6	7	8	9
10	11	12	13	14	15	16
17	18	19	20	21	22	23
24	25	26	27	28	29	30

DECEMBER 2024

S	M	T	W	T	F	S
1	2	3	4	5	6	7
8	9	10	11	12	13	14
15	16	17	18	19	20	21
22	23	24	25	26	27	28
29	30	31				

THIS WEEK'S
HAPPY MOMENT:

MONDAY
25

TUESDAY
26

IT'S COOL TO BE KIND!

WEDNESDAY
27

THURSDAY
28

BEING GRATEFUL FOR WHERE YOU ARE WILL GET YOU TO WHERE YOU'RE GOING.

Thanksgiving Day

FRIDAY
29

SPICE UP YOUR LIFE AND TRY SOMETHING NEW. IT MAY SURPRISE YOU!

SATURDAY
30

St. Andrew's Day (SCT)

SUNDAY
1

DON'T FORGET:

THIS WEEK'S HAPPY MOMENT:

NOVEMBER 2024

S	M	T	W	T	F	S
					1	2
3	4	5	6	7	8	9
10	11	12	13	14	15	16
17	18	19	20	21	22	23
24	25	26	27	28	29	30

DECEMBER 2024

S	M	T	W	T	F	S
1	2	3	4	5	6	7
8	9	10	11	12	13	14
15	16	17	18	19	20	21
22	23	24	25	26	27	28
29	30	31				

MONTHLY GOALS

NEW GOALS TO FOCUS ON

WHAT WORKED LAST MONTH

WHAT COULD BE BETTER

EVERYTHING STARTS WITH A dream

DECEMBER 2024

SUNDAY	MONDAY	TUESDAY	WEDNESDAY	THURSDAY	FRIDAY	SATURDAY
1	2	3	4	5	6	7 Pearl Harbor Day
8	9	10	11	12	13	14
15	16	17	18	19	20	21 Winter begins (Northern Hemisphere)
22	23	24 Christmas Eve	25 Christmas Day; Hanukkah begins	26 Kwanzaa begins; Boxing Day (AUS, CAN, NZ, UK)	27	28
29	30	31	1	2	3	4

CREATURE OF HABIT

Track new goals or habits and watch your progress every month!

HABIT	1	2	3	4	5	6	7	8	9	10	11	12	13	14	15	16	17	18	19	20	21	22	23	24	25	26	27	28	29	30	31

2024 DECEMBER

MONDAY
2

IF YOU'RE LOOKING FOR A SIGN, *THIS IS IT.*

TUESDAY
3

WEDNESDAY
4

LOVE YOURSELF FIRST.

THURSDAY
5

ICE CREAM IN DECEMBER? WHY NOT?

FRIDAY
6

SATURDAY
7

Pearl Harbor Day

HEALING IS
NOT LINEAR.

SUNDAY
8

DON'T FORGET:

DECEMBER 2024

S	M	T	W	T	F	S
1	2	3	4	5	6	7
8	9	10	11	12	13	14
15	16	17	18	19	20	21
22	23	24	25	26	27	28
29	30	31				

JANUARY 2025

S	M	T	W	T	F	S
			1	2	3	4
5	6	7	8	9	10	11
12	13	14	15	16	17	18
19	20	21	22	23	24	25
26	27	28	29	30	31	

THIS WEEK'S
HAPPY MOMENT:

2024 DECEMBER

MONDAY
9

TUESDAY
10

START YOUR DAY WITH A WARM DRINK AND A BIG SMILE

WEDNESDAY
11

THURSDAY
12

IT'S A WILD-RIDE LIFE.

FRIDAY
13

DIVE INTO COZY. HOT COCOA WILL HELP.

SATURDAY
14

SUNDAY
15

DON'T FORGET:

DECEMBER 2024

S	M	T	W	T	F	S
1	2	3	4	5	6	7
8	9	10	11	12	13	14
15	16	17	18	19	20	21
22	23	24	25	26	27	28
29	30	31				

JANUARY 2025

S	M	T	W	T	F	S
			1	2	3	4
5	6	7	8	9	10	11
12	13	14	15	16	17	18
19	20	21	22	23	24	25
26	27	28	29	30	31	

THIS WEEK'S HAPPY MOMENT:

2024 DECEMBER

MONDAY
16

DON'T STAND IN YOUR OWN WAY.

TUESDAY
17

WEDNESDAY
18

ACT WITH LOVE FIRST. REMEMBER THAT OTHERS MAY BE FACING STRUGGLES TOO.

THURSDAY
19

YOU ARE IN CHARGE OF BUILDING YOURSELF UP, NOT TEARING YOURSELF DOWN.

FRIDAY 20

SATURDAY 21

Winter begins (Northern Hemisphere)

YOU ARE NEVER TOO OLD TO BUILD A SNOWPERSON.

SUNDAY 22

DON'T FORGET:

DECEMBER 2024

S	M	T	W	T	F	S
1	2	3	4	5	6	7
8	9	10	11	12	13	14
15	16	17	18	19	20	21
22	23	24	25	26	27	28
29	30	31				

JANUARY 2025

S	M	T	W	T	F	S
			1	2	3	4
5	6	7	8	9	10	11
12	13	14	15	16	17	18
19	20	21	22	23	24	25
26	27	28	29	30	31	

THIS WEEK'S HAPPY MOMENT:

MONDAY
23

TUESDAY
24

GIVE THE GIFT OF THAT INCREDIBLE SMILE!

Christmas Eve

WEDNESDAY
25

Christmas Day; Hanukkah begins

THURSDAY
26

JOLLY AND JOYFUL!

Kwanzaa begins; Boxing Day (AUS, CAN, NZ, UK)

FRIDAY
27

YOU'RE NOT ALONE.

SATURDAY
28

SUNDAY
29

DON'T FORGET:

DECEMBER 2024

S	M	T	W	T	F	S
1	2	3	4	5	6	7
8	9	10	11	12	13	14
15	16	17	18	19	20	21
22	23	24	25	26	27	28
29	30	31				

JANUARY 2025

S	M	T	W	T	F	S
			1	2	3	4
5	6	7	8	9	10	11
12	13	14	15	16	17	18
19	20	21	22	23	24	25
26	27	28	29	30	31	

THIS WEEK'S
HAPPY MOMENT:

2024/25 DECEMBER/JANUARY

MONDAY
30

THROW YOUR PARTY PANTS ON!

TUESDAY
31

New Year's Eve

WEDNESDAY
1

CHEERS TO A NEW YEAR OF BEING YOU!

New Year's Day

THURSDAY
2

Day after New Year's Day (NZ, SCT)

BLOOM ON YOUR OWN TIME.

FRIDAY
3

SATURDAY
4

GET STARTED BY
GETTING STARTED.

SUNDAY
5

DON'T FORGET:

DECEMBER 2024

S	M	T	W	T	F	S
1	2	3	4	5	6	7
8	9	10	11	12	13	14
15	16	17	18	19	20	21
22	23	24	25	26	27	28
29	30	31				

JANUARY 2025

S	M	T	W	T	F	S
			1	2	3	4
5	6	7	8	9	10	11
12	13	14	15	16	17	18
19	20	21	22	23	24	25
26	27	28	29	30	31	

THIS WEEK'S
HAPPY MOMENT:

NOTES AND INSPIRATION

Jewish and Muslim holidays begin at sundown.

Published by Sourcebooks.
P.O. Box 4410, Naperville, Illinois 60567-4410
(630) 961-3900
sourcebooks.com

Printed and bound in China.
OGP 10 9 8 7 6 5 4 3 2 1